I AM MY Affirmations

A Coloring Book To Empower Women & Girls All Over The World

By: Rockell Bartoli

Thank You

Thank you to Sasha O'Hara for your amazing support and guidance. Also, to my family and friends who enjoyed this process with me.

Dedication

This book is dedicated to every special women and girl who will color it and believe it. You are wonderful!

Copyright © 2017 Rockell Bartoli, LLC
All Rights Reserved. No parts of this publication may be reproduced, distributed or transmitted in any form or by any means, including photocopying, recording, or other electronic or mechanical methods, without the prior written permission of the publisher

www.rockellbartoli.com

I AM STRONG

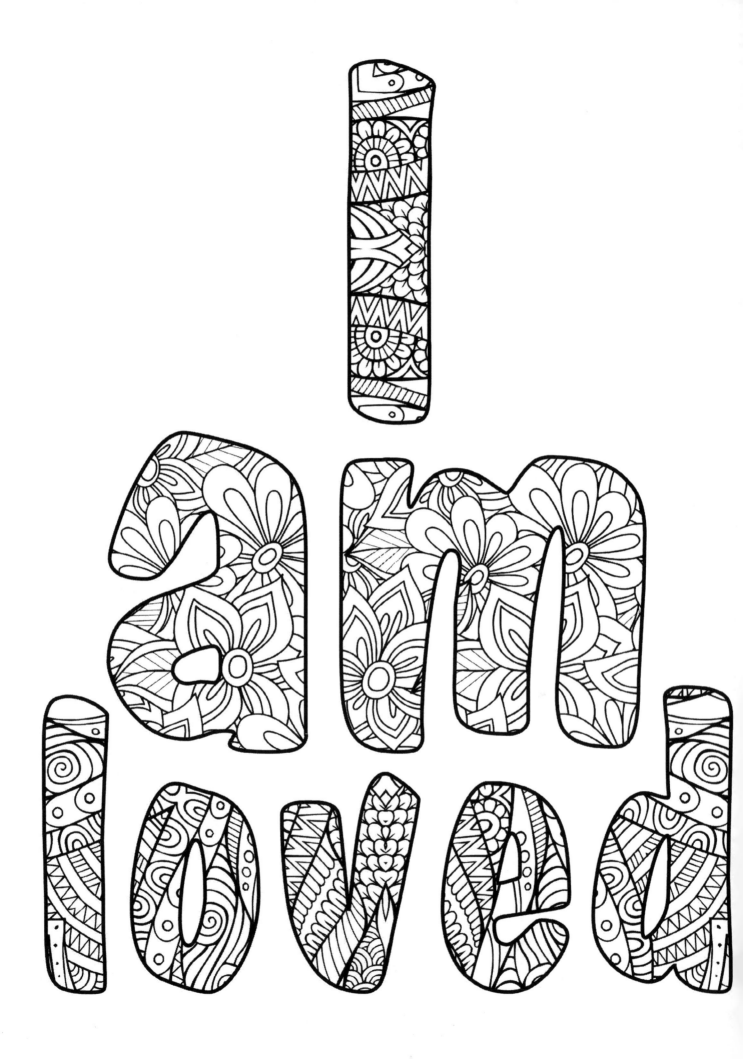

I AM FIERCE

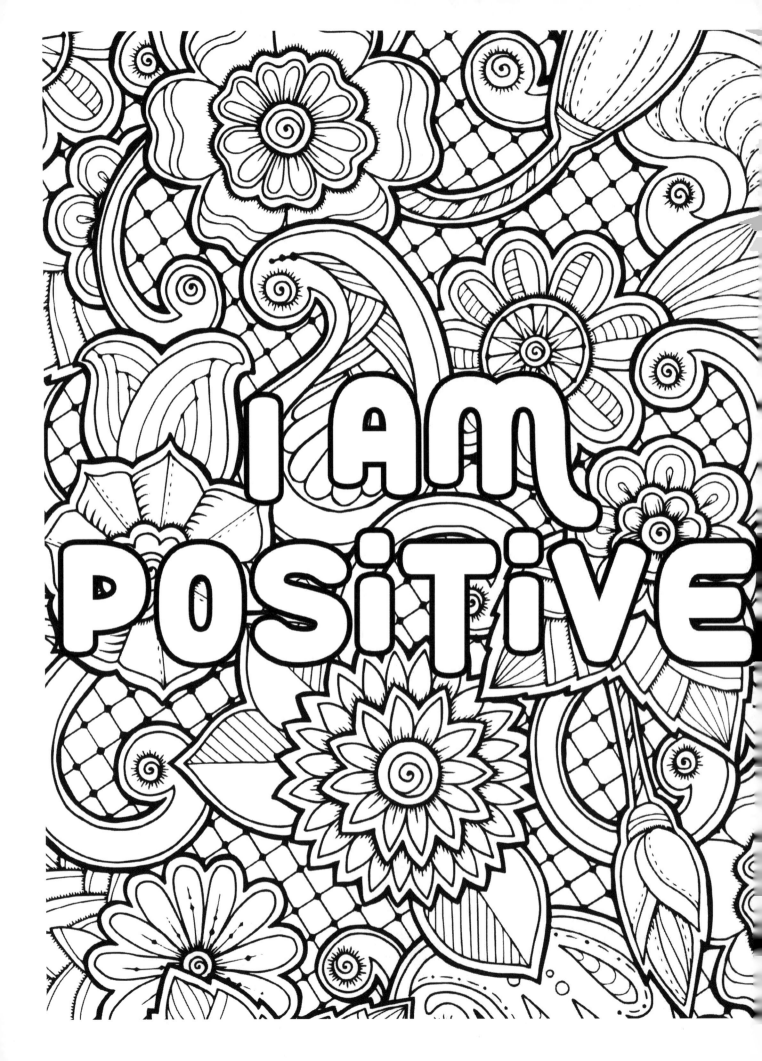

I am happy

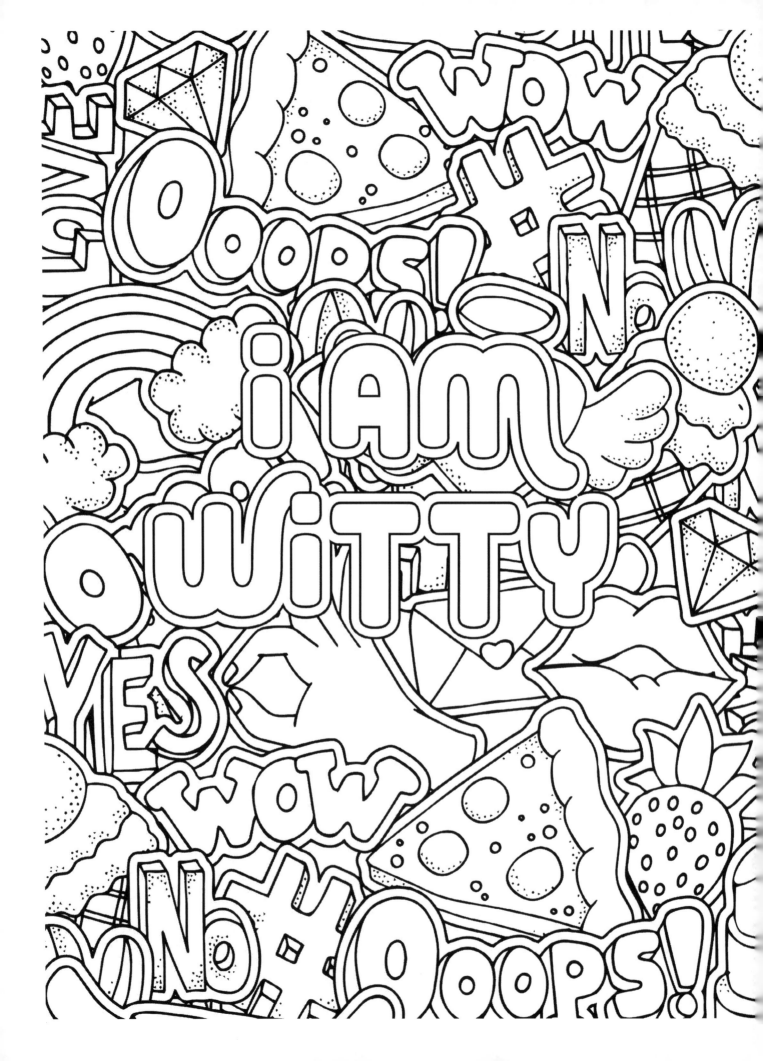

I AM SUCCESS

Made in the USA
Coppell, TX
26 September 2020